Managing Mental Health for Gender Dysphoria

Discover How You Can Overcome Depression and Anxiety on Your Own

J.M. Dominique

Table of Contents

Introduction

Shaun had always felt that he was different from other people. He often envied his classmates as they strut off the senior high school grounds, laughing and goofing around, comfortable in their own skin. He often wondered if they too experienced the things he was undergoing. It was difficult to confide in anybody, and Shaun felt his secret wasn't safe to tell anyone. The guidance counselor kept on prodding him, gently but repeatedly to the point of being annoying, to confide in her. But Shaun didn't budge, giving only a few nods and a lot of silence when summoned one day to the counselor's office. Shaun's secret wasn't easy to explain, let alone for

Shaun to understand himself. You see, Shaun thought he was a she.

He was born with male organs and raised up as a boy. Shaun was the pride of his father. As the first boy in the family, everyone doted on him, giving him blue clothes, gifting him with toy guns and cars, painting his room blue. He may not have good memories of his childhood, but Shaun could remember being forced to cut his hair short and wear pants. At school, Shaun dreaded playing sports. It wasn't because he was not good in basketball; he just didn't like the roughness of the other boys. He'd rather play jumping ropes with the rest of the girls. He didn't have too many boy friends because Shaun knew he enjoyed the company of girls more.

Because of this, Shaun was thoroughly bullied in school. He had a lot of nicknames in school, ranging from 'fag' to 'closet' to 'Miss Prude' and even 'Cinderella man'. Name-calling wasn't the end of it. Shaun experienced having his bag stolen only to be found at the garbage can.

When he walked through the cafeteria, it wasn't uncommon for him to be splashed with orange juice or anything yucky and slimy. Shaun had transferred twice already, with a thought that the new school would be different from the previous. But Shaun knew all schools harbored bullies and there was no rest for him. He would often stay in the bathroom for hours just to avoid being pranked by the other kids.

He was good at Math, but he often had low grades. Shaun's mother had been summoned by the teacher, only to explain how Shaun had a lot of potential he wasn't reflecting on his grades. Shaun would only nod and keep silent about the whole thing. He liked Math after all, but he couldn't study for it, thinking of all the bullies that would rip his homework as soon as the class started. High school was probably the worst part of his life, and Shaun knew this was going to continue for a long time.

Shaun would often draw just to escape from everything. He liked designing dresses for weddings. He had a handy notebook with him and on his free time, he would sketch all the bridal gown ideas that would come to him. Shaun often imagined wearing a long gown. He knew how tight the gown had to be, how it would fit his waist and hug his chest, showing some skin but never bordering on cheap and distasteful. Shaun knew he wanted to be free enough to wear that beautiful gown, wear it proud in the streets, and wear it for all the world to see. Shaun wanted to be free, especially from his manly body. Shaun knew he was a girl, but his body wasn't cooperating.

Lost and alone, Shaun didn't know where to turn to. There were bullies everywhere and he was tired from getting punched, tripped and sloshed. He didn't trust adults too much because they would often chide him to 'straighten his act together.' His friends were all in his first school and they probably had other friends by now. Shaun felt so depressed that he even thought of ending his life. It did not matter if he died. Perhaps he would be born again in a woman's body. That would mean the world to Shaun. But he just couldn't do it. Shaun felt alone, trapped and depressed. Was there anyone who can help him? Was there anyone who can understand him?

You may have probably read or bought this book because you were able to relate to Shaun's experience. Shaun, not his real name, is based on an actual person who was very much confused and dissatisfied with his gender. You may have had similar thoughts like him and often wished someone was out there to understand you. Like Shaun, you may have thought that you were the only one having those feelings of alienation in your body. There are even those who have married already, with children in tow. And then, in their adulthood, they begin to express their discomfort with their gender. This book is for you.

Or you might have friends who are like Shaun. They may be timid and reclusive, often alone and having difficulty socializing with everyone. Or you may know of people who cross-dress, not out of fun, but because they think that they are wearing their true clothes. They may be co-workers who have difficulty going to the bathroom because the labels don't resonate with who they are. And you worry a lot about them. You don't understand them at all, but you just want to help them find understanding and peace. This book is for you.

Or you may just be curious about people in general. You may know of transgenders and transsexuals and you are fascinated at how they transitioned. Deviant behavior may intrigue you and you just want to understand their condition, their way of thinking, their way of behaving. The world we live in is growing in complexity, including the blurring of gender and sex lines. It is an age characterized by gender fluidity, political correctness and surgical reorientation. You may simply want to learn more about how this age thinks and behaves in order to anticipate the kind of culture we are going to create in the next generations. This book is for you.

I hope that this book helps those who feel alone and trapped in their physical bodies. I hope that many people will understand your condition. I hope that this book becomes a safe space to talk about sex, gender and mental health. The issue of gender dysphoria may be misunderstood by a lot of people, yet it exists. I hope that together, we can provide an understanding space where everyone can be themselves. This book will take you to a journey to understanding gender dysphoria and how to take care of your mental health and allow you to help those who feel alone, trapped and misunderstood.

Chapter 1: Understanding Gender Dysphoria

One of the emerging issues of this generation is gender dysphoria. You may have heard something about it, as popularized by movies or blogs or other forms of social media. You may hear the term being used around by your classmates, co-workers, friends, siblings of any age and background. Or you have felt gender dysphoric yourself. Or you may have had the feeling of gender dysphoria, but not exactly know that it is the term for what you are feeling. Regardless of your background, you are here because there is something you want to learn more about gender dysphoria.

In the Diagnostic and Statistical Manual of Mental Disorders (DSM-V) from the American Psychiatric Association defines gender dysphoria as the feeling of discomfort a person feels when their gender at birth is contrary to the one they identify with. The term 'dysphoria' refers to the unease or dissatisfaction with a certain state of life. And gender dysphoria refers to the general unease in the difference between your given gender and the one you identify with. These statements need much unpacking and that entails further definition of certain terms. We need to be very careful with definitions because the use of words and terms are very open to misunderstanding and multiple interpretations, leading to much confusion.

First, we need to define the difference between 'sex' and 'gender'. These two terms are often interchangeably used which is very irresponsible. To set the record clear, the American Psychiatric Association defines sex as the "biological indicators of male and female, understood in the context of reproductive capacity, such as in sex chromosomes, gonads, sex hormones and non-ambiguous internal and external genitalia." When we say that the 'sex of a person' is male, we are referring to their being born with a penis, having the chromosome of XY, having pubic or facial hair, having testes and produce sperm. When we refer to a person's sex as female, we refer to her identity as being born with an XX chromosome, having a uterus, a vagina, ovulating monthly, having protruding breasts.   To define sex further, we can differentiate between primary and secondary sexual characteristics. These refer to the biological manifestations of a person as male or female. Primary refers to the reproductive organs of a person. For males, this is a penis; for the girls, the vagina. Secondary characteristics refer to the non-sexual characteristics that define a male and a female. Secondary characteristics are the result of the distinct predominant hormones in a person. These may include facial hair and a low voice for males as a result of testosterone and enlarged breasts and softer voices as a result of estrogen in females. This needs to be clear that sex is a biological feature because there will be a lot of misunderstanding when we introduce the concept of gender later.

We emphasize here that the sex of a person is defined at birth. This is because people may choose to undergo sexual reassignment, which is a sex change, where their primary and secondary characteristics may be changed. A person born a man, may choose to have a 'vagina' formed through surgery. But we still define the sex of a person based on the chromosome and the reproductive capacity of that person. You may have formed a new vagina, but you still have XY chromosomes, making your sex still a male sex.

We take note also of abnormalities in sexual development. There are people who may be born with ambiguous sex such as hermaphrodites. People with Turner Syndrome for example are born with XO or a missing chromosome. They are genetically females but they exhibit male features. People with Klinefelter syndrome are born with chromosome XXY. They are male but they may exhibit female features and may be infertile. These abnormalities in sexual development may predispose individuals to gender dysphoria since their sexual characteristics may be glaringly different or ambivalent to the gender assigned to them or to their preferred gender. If these sexual abnormalities are not addressed, whether medically or surgically, these individuals have a higher risk of gender dysphoria.

Gender, on the other hand, refers to the "lived role in society and/or the identification as male or female." These roles are socially and psychologically constructed, creating norms specific to the gender. The key term here is 'socially constructed' which means that each culture appropriates a certain set of behaviors and norms that define what it means to be a male or a female. For example, a certain culture may designate the wearing of pants for boys and the wearing of skirts for girls. There are 'masculine' types of work such as carpentry or hunting or driving. There are also 'feminine' types of work such as cooking, embroidery or dressmaking. These designations are a product of biological, psychological and social factors. Men are physically bigger and stronger, thus they are able to do most manual labors more effectively. Women are more sensitive and caring, thus they are more apt for nurturing kinds of work. These norms are constructed, thus they are specific to the culture and time of a certain society. The norms may change, though not drastically, through time. If before, only men can wear pants, we see that today, it is acceptable for anyone to wear pants. It is socially acceptable now for women to engage in some typically male lines of work such as driving or manufacturing. The norms then are subject to change depending on the openness of each society. We see how these changes unfold historically, with norms being challenged and negotiated across time. The Victorian woman was deemed as prim and proper, knowledgeable in the arts and trained in dancing and in good manners, passive to their husbands. The 21st century woman is independent and willful, can be single if she wanted to, able to choose whichever profession she sets her heart to, speaks her mind and fights for her cause. Husbands before are the breadwinners of the family, working in the field and bringing the income home. Now, the wife too can work, can hold a profession and bring in income, while the husband may also stay at home to take care of the children. Gender and gender roles are socially determined. The gender of a person also constitutes a legal identity, wherein an individual is legally recognized as male or female.

At birth then, people are assigned a gender based on their sex. This is also called the 'natal gender'. If you have a penis, then you are designated to be male, while if you have a vagina, you are designated as female. As designated males and females then, individuals are raised to follow the social norms assigned to each gender. Boys are raised to like the color blue, to play with toy cars, to be rough and strong, not to cry when hurt and play basketball or football. Girls are raised to like the color pink, to be sensitive and dainty, and to play with dolls and jumping ropes, to be obedient and smart. Parents try to raise their children in the manner appropriate for the social roles of male and female. And as we grow older, we try to conform to these norms, constructing our own version of what it means to be male and female.

Gender dysphoria then is born from an incongruence between one's preferred gender and the gender assigned to you at birth and by society. Preference marks the independence of an individual in identifying with a particular gender and all the designations that come with that. You may be born to a gender, but your personal preference does not match that particular assigned gender. The DSM-V emphasizes that the illness is not found in the gender of the person, but in the increasing anxiety and distress that follows the incongruence. Being gay or homosexual or transgender is not per se a mental illness. Rather, the distress in not having the physical and social characteristics of your desired gender constitutes the mental disorder we want to address.

The DSM-V goes in to categorize gender dysphoria according to age groups. It has a different set of criteria for evaluating children, adolescents and adults. This is a sound evaluation because it takes into account both the physical and socio-emotional development of people. Adolescence marks the period of great physical changes in our bodies because of the influence of hormones. The transition from childhood to adolescence to adulthood then marks dramatic changes in our skin, hair, voice, and body. With these physical changes comes the growing consciousness of individuals to assert their own authority over their bodies. Children may not have much choice over the types of toys they play with or the school they go to. Adults may have more means to pay for hormonal medication or surgical procedures to suit their choices. Preference then is born out of a recognition of what we personally want, and what our body and society tell us. Hence, it is more prudent to characterize gender dysphoria as it occurs in the developmental phases.

Children begin to express gender dysphoria as early as 2 to 4 years of age. Boys for gender dysphoria express these distresses and attempts at resolving the distress in different domains. In terms of clothes, they would like to wear dresses or choose feminine colors like pink or red. They may even play with drapes or towels or curtains to fashion themselves dresses. They would try to grow their hair long and experiment with different types of feminine hairstyles. In terms of toys and recreation, they would rather play with dolls and cooking ware. They would pretend to assume the role of a mother in make-believe fantasy role-playing, cooking for their tiny dolls, feeding the dolls or washing their clothes. They may hate rough games like contact sports and basketball, often missing out on PE classes or preferring to play skipping ropes after school. They would experiment with lipstick and make-up, often borrowing their mother's beauty kits in secret. When urinating, they would train themselves to pee while sitting down. Some may even be disgusted at having a penis, finding it gross to look at. They may even adopt a female name.

Girls with gender dysphoria, on the other hand, may exhibit the opposite features. They may prefer wearing pants or shorts instead of skirts. They may hate long hair and prefer to cut it short. They may be heavy into sports, doing well in football or basketball, even at par with the boys. Some may try to pee while standing up, and some even express a desire not to have developed breasts and to menstruate.

Adolescence represents the age of sexual maturation and experimenting. Here, the hormonal imbalances lead to dramatic changes in the body especially the hair, the voice, the built and height, the primary and secondary sexual characteristics. Girls will start having their menstruation and development of their breasts. Boys will develop lower voices, bigger shoulders and more mature sexual organs. Both sexes will develop hair on various parts of their bodies. Gender dysphoria may be very intense then on this stage as individuals struggle sociopsychologically with these physical changes. Boys may shave their legs or their armpit and bind their penises so it won't bulge. Girls would bind their breasts. Both genders will try to have access to hormonal medication to ease the distress they are experiencing in the hopes of becoming more of their preferred gender.

These distresses may be outgrown as people becomes socialized. The distress may even just be transient, disappearing as adolescents' transition into adulthood. But for some, the distress may persist and carry over to adulthood.

Dysphoria occurring in childhood and carried over to adulthood are called early-onset gender dysphoria. This occurs more commonly than its latter counterpart. Parents may detect this early or the children themselves may verbally express this. Some adults on the other hand, may develop dysphoria only when they are much older. The dysphoria could occur in their pubertal years or even late into their adulthood. Their parents may not have an inkling or they themselves may have led ordinary childhoods. But when the distress only manifests in adulthood, this is called a late-onset gender dysphoria.

Gender dysphoria in adulthood may be due to the persistence of the distress from their childhood years, a new occurrence or a repressed one. They may be more vocal about their opinions and preferences in identifying with the opposite gender. Coping styles of individuals to ease the distress are expressed in a variety of ways. Some may go full out in transvestic behavior, cross-dressing to match their preferred identity. Some may resort to hormonal medication, to enhance breast development for males and to increase hair in females. The adoption of an opposite gender name may develop into a full personality, even using gender-preferred pronouns to refer to themselves. If the distress is not resolved, some may even go for surgical measures.

In terms of attraction, having gender dysphoria increases the likelihood of being attracted to the same sex. This is especially true in early-onset gender dysphoria. There is sexual excitement upon interacting with people of the same sex. In late-onset gender dysphoria, while the majority do adopt a homosexual identity or an attraction to the same sex, some may have had sexual relations of the opposite sex. It is not uncommon for some late-onset gender dysphoric individuals to have previously conventional lives of being married with a spouse and even siring children. When the dysphoria hits them, they may begin to identify as either gay or lesbian, or may even stay in the marriage, adopting the role of the opposite gender.

What causes gender dysphoria? Studies show that the cause of dysphoria involves the confluence of temperamental, environmental, genetic, physiological and cultural factors. Those who display gender atypical behavior earlier on in their childhood have a higher chance of manifesting it in their adulthood.

The environment at home may also play a factor. Males with gender dysphoria may have older brothers and may have been raised more femininely. Mothers for example who desire a daughter but only have sons may tend to raise one of them as female, giving them clothes or calling them by a feminine name. Fathers may contribute to the stress as they may not be supportive of the individual's distress.

The school environment may also be very stressful for the individual with gender dysphoria. There is a strong urge to conform to gender stereotypes of being male or female. Deviations from the norm may lead to bullying which increases the distress. Some adolescents may feel threatened to even go to school, participate in activities such as PE where they have to conform to gender assigned activities, be discriminated on their hairstyle and fashion. With a threatening environment, the distress may carry over to adulthood.

There are studies that try to explore the contribution of genetics on gender dysphoria. Studies on twins provide some link between the occurrences of transsexuals on monozygotic twins. But overall, there is insufficient evidence to pinpoint any one gene that could explain the occurrence of gender dysphoria. Since most individuals with gender dysphoria fail to procreate given their sexual attraction for the same sex, there seems to be no sufficient evidence to prove that gender dysphoria is passed on through generations. But for those with mental illnesses like depression or anxiety disorders, these conditions may be genetically be inherited.

If individuals then with gender dysphoria have mental illnesses along their family history, the stress they feel from the incongruence may exacerbate or increase the risk of occurrence of the inherited mental disorders.

Cultural studies show the prevalence of gender dysphoria across countries and cultures. Since each culture will appropriate their particular set of norms assigned to each gender, there will be individuals who will not fit those categories. But since culture is a mix of stability and fluidity, these norms will also be in a constant state of flux. The status of gender dysphoria then will vary in degree according to the permissiveness of cultures.

In summary, gender dysphoria occurs because of the combined influences of the personality, the environment and upbringing, genetics and culture. Each domain contributes to the incongruence as individuals appropriate the norms set by society to their context. Further studies need to explore how strongly each domain contributes to the prevalence of gender dysphoria.

Chapter 2: Symptoms of Gender Dysphoria

How do we know that someone has gender dysphoria? Are there physical signs we can observe? Is having gender dysphoria a cause for alarm? After reading chapter 1, you may already have some inkling on what gender dysphoria is. But before you can start diagnosing people, it is important to gauge if the incongruence people feel about their assigned and preferred gender is something transitory or really enduring. The duration of the symptoms is all important in the diagnosis of gender dysphoria.

The DSM-V has set the criteria for diagnosing gender dysphoria. What is good in this manual is that it takes into consideration the age and maturity of individuals. Each age group has a specific set of criteria that will help in identifying people with gender dysphoria.

According to DSM-V, gender dysphoria or the stress one feels when there is a disparity between the assigned versus the preferred gender is diagnosed in children if the child feels at least 6 of the following symptoms for a minimum of a 6-month duration:

1. A strong desire to be of the other gender
2. A preference for cross-dressing (wearing clothes typically assigned to the opposite gender)
3. A strong preference for cross-gender roles when engaged in fantasy play
4. Preference for playmates of the opposite gender
5. A preference for the typically assigned toys (guns and robots for boys and dolls and cookware for girls) or activities of the opposite gender

6. A rejection of toys and activities of the assigned gender

7. A strong dislike of one's anatomy

8. A strong desire to acquire the primary and secondary characteristics of the other gender.

There should also be significant impairment in the different domains of functioning such as school, family or among peers. When we say impairment, the child experiences severe distress regarding his or her gender that leads him to not do well in school, get into frequent fights, withdraw from social events, or even attempt suicide. In terms of the family dynamics, you have to watch out if the child is becoming more reclusive or secretive or often gets into fights with his or her siblings. These impairments are not just mild or of small consequences. Gender dysphoria may affect one or more important domains, increasing the distress of individuals.

We emphasize the need to look at these symptoms across more than 6 months duration.

We want to establish that these tendencies leading to impairments are chronic, occurring throughout a long period of time. Children may express dislike of their anatomy one time, and then forget about it at another. This is simply transitory and may not qualify for a diagnosis of gender dysphoria. It may then be more appropriate to call these as episodes of gender dysphoria. When diagnosing, we want to establish the distress as enduring conditions, and not simply the whims of children that come and go. You have to be sure when the first symptoms occurred, if it is recurring in a regular interval and the current status of the child. It is important to know the duration because this will also determine the intervention needed. For children who express these symptoms for less than 6 months, then observation is the only intervention appropriate. We only need to closely observe these children and monitor if the symptoms persist longer. But for those who have symptoms occurring for at least 6 months or more, then there should be active intervention. We will discuss more of these in the next chapters.

Close observation is needed more in children than in adolescents or in adults because of the incapacity of children to fully express themselves and their preferences. They may show some distress, but they may have problems verbalizing them. For example, your child may not say that he or she dislikes his or her sexual organs. But when you bathe them, they may show signs of disgust when they are looking at their own organs. Or, some children may not be comfortable opening up to their parents about being bullied at school. You will only see that they have a problem when a major event, such as detention or failing in subjects, have already occurred.

For adolescents and adults, the DSM-V has a separate criteria, recognizing the growing independence of individuals and their capacity to be self-reflective and expressive of their preferences. Again, we note that the symptoms should have been seen for at least 6 months. For adolescents and adults to be diagnosed with gender dysphoria, they must exhibit at least two of the following symptoms:

1. A marked incongruence between one's experienced gender and primary and/or secondary sexual characteristics.
2. A strong desire to be rid of one's primary and/or secondary sexual characteristics
3. A strong desire to obtain the primary and/or secondary sexual characteristics of the opposite gender
4. A strong desire to be of the other gender
5. A strong desire to be treated like the other gender
6. A strong conviction that one has the typical feelings and reactions of the other gender

Again, these symptoms must lead the individual to have an impairment in the major domains of their life. The distress may cause them not to do well at work or even to fail to find work, establish friendships and sexual relations, develop depressive attitudes and anti-social behavior or impede their concentration, sleep or appetite. If the duration and the symptoms are established, then intervention is necessary. Otherwise, close observation is warranted.

We need to unpack some of the DSM-V criteria on diagnosing adolescents and adults because some of them may not be self-explanatory. The DSM-V is not just repeating the same thing over and over. Each criterion tackles a different aspect of a person and are distinct and mutually exclusive. For example, there will be individuals who will only exhibit 2 out of the 6 criteria. They may want to be of the other gender and be treated like the other gender, but they may not want to be rid of their anatomical parts. At least 2 of the 6 criteria have to be met in order to diagnose gender dysphoria.

The first criterion talks about distress. The incongruence must bring about significant stress to the person. The second talks about dislike for one's own sexual characteristics. This could refer to the dislike of a male for his penis and his low voice or hairiness. For a female, this could be an aversion to her vagina and breasts, a desire to be rid of them. The third looks at the other gender's sexual characteristic. A female may want to have a penis or to have more hair on themselves. The fourth is more generally stated as a desire for the other gender. This means going beyond the physical aspects to the entire personality and characteristics of the other gender. A male wants to be a woman or a female wants to be a man. The fifth moves out from the self to the treatment of society on one's preferred gender. This may include the use of politically correct pronouns. A male who wants to be female might prefer to be referred as a 'she'. The last criterion goes back to the self in reference to the other gender's typical manifestations of feelings. A female who wants to be a man will try to act rough and callous, as is typical of men. Though the criteria may be similar, they discuss different aspects of the experience of gender dysphoria.

Chapter 3: Effects of Gender Dysphoria to Your Mental Health

In discussing mental health, we have to reiterate the point that desiring to be of the other gender is not in itself a mental disorder. Being gay, lesbian or homosexual is also not a mental illness. The DSM-V emphasizes that identity is not a disorder but pinpoints rather the distress that comes from the incongruence between assigned and preferred gender. Along with the stress, comes a host of other mental illnesses.

We also have to point out here that the stress required in diagnosing gender dysphoria is of a degree that impairs personal and social functioning at important domains in your life. Stress is not in itself a disorder. There is a range of degrees of stresses that may not necessarily be a mental illness. You are stressed when you miss the bus. You feel stressed when you break up with someone that you love. You feel stressed when your boss berates you. There are different kinds of stress that we feel on a daily basis. But the diagnosis of gender dysphoria is only met when the stress fulfills two criteria: it must be enduring and is felt for at least 6 months and that it impairs your functioning in different domains. Anything less than that are simply part of daily stresses or bordering on clinical gender dysphoria. But intervention will only be entertained when those two criteria are met. This means that the individual is experiencing severe stress that will require management.

In general, mental health refers to the quality of your mental status that is able to function on important domains of your life. Much of medicine has been previously focused only on the somatic conditions. You are sick because you have a tummy ache or you have chest pain. These would require medications or surgeries to address the problem on the body. But the advent of psychology and neurology has opened the field for mental health. Over the past century, people are recognizing mental health disorders as distinct and important aspects of the overall health of people. They may accompany somatic disorders. For example, you have been diagnosed with cancer, and that affects your outlook on life. The somatic part, the cancer affecting your body, also affects your mental health, which will lead you to think negatively or entertain morbid thoughts. But mental health can also lead to somatic disorders. Depressive people may forget to eat properly leading to anorexia or nutritional imbalances. We have to recognize that mental health is important and that taking care of it should be a priority.

As such, certain disorders of mental health accompany people who have been diagnosed with gender dysphoria. Again, the wisdom of the DSM-V is that it approaches gender dysphoria from a developmental perspective. The mental disorders that may co-occur with gender dysphoria are distinct between children and adolescents and adults. Their contexts are entirely different, reflecting different accompanying mental disorders and subsequent interventions. But we can also say that some mental disorders from childhood that are not addressed may be carried over to adulthood. These disorders persist and may be difficult to correct the longer they are not addressed.

In children diagnosed with gender dysphoria, we can see great lability in terms of emotional and behavioral problems. As children not coming in terms with their gender, they are prone to being bullied and ostracized by their peers. The bullying then may trigger symptoms of depression or anxiety among children. They may withdraw from school activities, lose sleep or sleep most of the time, and have difficulty in engaging in friendships. If not addressed, some may even slip into severe depression leading to suicidal ideation and even attempts.

Adolescents and adults, on the other hand, will experience two general mental disorders accompanying and contributing to gender dysphoria. These may be remnants of their childhood trauma, but they may also independently occur. We will discuss how anxiety and depression work and how they significantly impact the quality of life of people with gender dysphoria.

First, depression refers to the low and negative mood of a person. We can distinguish it from mere sadness from the duration and intensity of the depressed mood. Sadness can simply be transient. You are sad that the sky is dark. You are sad that a friend has illness. You are sad that you got demoted from work. Depression, on the other hand, is more enduring and affects the functioning of a person. It is a more intense kind of sadness because it persists for a longer period of time and that you fail to function well on many parts of your life.

Specifically, the DSM-V enumerates certain criteria to diagnose a Major Depressive Disorder (MDD). The golden period we are looking for here is two weeks, which means that the symptoms must be present for at least two weeks. In order to diagnose a major depressive disorder, you must exhibit at least five of the nine criteria. Out of those five, one of them must be either the first or the second criteria. The following symptoms for MDD are as follows:

1. Depressed mood during the day which may be self-reported or observed by others.
2. Diminished interest or pleasure in the activities of the day
3. Weight loss or weight gain (of 5% of the total body weight for each month) or increase or decrease in appetite.
4. Increase or decrease in the amount of sleep

5. Agitation or retardation during most of the day

6. Fatigue or a feeling of tiredness everyday

7. Having feelings of guilt or worthlessness inappropriate to an occasion everyday

8. Decrease in the ability to think or concentrate

9. Recurring thoughts of death and dying.

How does a person with gender dysphoria experience this? One key insight here is the capacity of our thoughts to influence our feelings and moods. When there is incongruence between what gender you are assigned to and what gender you prefer, you may think about yourself negatively. You may think that you are not enough and that you should be in another body and gender altogether. You may also think negatively about the world. You are surrounded by bullies at school or at work. Even going to a restroom may also trigger you to think that the world is judging you by forcing you to pick a side you have been assigned to. Or you may think that your situation is hopeless, that no matter how much you change your hair or wear a skirt, people will always see you as different or as your assigned gender. These negative thoughts about yourself, the world and the future all contribute to the net effect of a depressed mood.

By thinking about that and letting the depressed mood pervade, you may begin to experience less pleasure. If normally you find going to the gym a relaxing and pleasurable activity, you may now feel threatened as if everybody is watching you. Binging on your favorite food may have been an addiction, but when you are depressed, everything tastes bland. This is especially important to note because if you have decreased pleasure, you will seek different and often risky types of pleasure. Depressed people with gender dysphoria are at a higher risk for substance abuse such as alcohol and drugs. These abuses are in themselves mental disorders that could contribute to the stress you are feeling. What is dangerous in substance abuse is that you can overdo the consumption of these substances just to get your high and you may end up with a somatic disease or even death.

Weight and appetite are also factors we need to observe when dealing with depression in gender dysphoria. Food triggers certain pleasure hormones in the body like endorphins. You eat chocolate, and you feel happy. Because of the fluctuating moods in gender dysphoria, individuals may undergo two extremities, both of them overdoing it. On one hand, they may start binging on food just to get pleasure. You feel so depressed and judged by society because of your gender so you start eating and eating and eating. If you don't watch it, this can actually cause obesity and increased risk for cardiovascular diseases. On the other hand, you may lose all pleasure from eating so that you eat less and less and less. From obesity, you can swing now to anorexia, leading to a lot of nutritional deficiencies. Take note when you have changes in weight and appetite when you are undergoing stressful deliberations in gender dysphoria.

Another source of pleasure and relaxation that is prone to abuse is sleep. When you are stressed, it is either you sleep too much or sleep too little. Good sleep is not a matter of hours, because it will vary for individuals. There are some who are contented with four hours of sleep, some cannot go without six hours. What is important here is that you feel rested. If you are depressed, you may lose sleep because you keep on thinking about your incongruence and what others think about you. Lack of sleep will predispose you to palpitations and fatigue and a lot of hormonal imbalances. On the other hand, depressed people with gender dysphoria may also oversleep. Instead of confronting their work or socializing with friends, they would rather stay at home and sleep the day away. When asked about the quality of their sleep, they would reply that they still feel tired after taking 10 hours of sleep.

You have to be observant of these sleeping patterns.

The incongruence and depression may also bring about either agitation or retardation. You feel on edge the whole day. Every little mistake, every unexpected turn of events may startle you. There is a feeling of being attacked at all sides because you are different from all the others. Or, you may simply feel drained and refuse to budge. The hopelessness of your situation may just immobilize you, paralyzing you from doing any productive activity. You'd rather stay home than do work or go to school. You don't let feelings run through you because you just want to numb out the world. Be wary when gender dysphoric people are too panicky or having too much flat affect. Flat affect is when there is a severe reduction in emotional expressiveness. This may be a danger sign to watch out for.

People who are depressed may also feel very tired after a long day. This is felt even if you really didn't do anything physically. You may have just stayed at home, sitting on your sofa, and you still feel exhausted. You may be physically rested, but since your mind is running back and forth, nurturing your distress and incongruence, you still feel tired. Much of the battle is in the mind, and that is where the person with gender dysphoria feels most drained from.

People with depression may also feel excessive and even inappropriate guilt or feelings of worthlessness. Bullying may ingrain that sense of worthlessness in you that you cannot shake off. You are a male but you want to be female and you cannot do anything about it. That helplessness makes you think lowly about yourself. You will never be the woman you want to become. That thought crushes you and feeds the depression.

Thinking too much also accompanies depression. The incongruence is played out in the mind and you are bombarded with different negative thoughts. There is a tendency to overthink because of the feeling of worthlessness. You think about how others will perceive you.

There is a preoccupation on getting approval from others. You think of the many ways you can be more like the gender you want to be. This thinking will eat up your time that you cannot concentrate on any other tasks. Instead of finishing your presentations for a meeting, you are stuck thinking about what your colleagues will think of your clothes. Instead of writing that accounting report, you are worrying about the unwanted hair you have on your face. Too much thinking spirals down to negative thinking, perpetuating your depressed mood.

And finally, depressed people may also entertain thoughts of death and dying. If you are not able to become the gender you want to be, the only resolve you might think of is to kill yourself or to die. This is the most dangerous symptoms because there is an increased risk of suicidal ideation that could lead to an attempt. You cannot disregard this symptom or the other classical signs of depression because a life might be at stake if you miss out on this.

The other mental disorder that may accompany gender dysphoria is anxiety. Like, depression, anxiety is also concerned with a lot of thinking and worrying. They may actually overlap and co-exist along with gender dysphoria. Anxiety may also be similar to trauma in the intensity of worrying in anticipation of future events. We feel anxious or traumatized by something that has not happened but may happen to us. In order to differentiate the two, we say that in trauma, the worry is about an event that is specific, say heights or snakes or open spaces. In anxiety, you don't worry about singular events, but you are just panicky with the general situation. The object of worry in anxiety is non-specific.

In the DSM-V, the criteria for diagnosing a person with generalized anxiety disorder is having three out of the following six symptoms:

1. Restlessness or feeling on edge
2. Easy fatigability
3. Difficulty concentrating

4. Irritability

5. Muscle tension

6. Sleep disturbance.

We have discussed some of the criteria above in depression and they also hold true for anxiety. But we can highlight some of the unique features of anxiety here. One, irritability can be seen in anxious people when they are stressed with little details. If you have gender dysphoria, you may overthink everything that even the slightest annoying details may set off your mood. You may be concentrating at work and a small error on your report may set you off screaming at an employee. A car may cut you off on the road, and you just want to run him over as you chase him through the highway. A waiter brings you the wrong food and you dress him down in public. The irritation is not appropriate to the situation. You already feel tensed from worrying about your gender. And you carry that tension to other areas of your life, affecting your work and your performance.

Muscle tension represents the somatic manifestation of the stress. You feel back pains, arm pains, stomach pains, foot pains, pains all over your body because of the stress you feel. Stress releases a lot of hormones like norepinephrine and adrenaline that increase your metabolism, priming your body to fight or fly from the problem. This is important when you have an emergency or an impending danger. But it should subside when the danger is out of sight. When you have gender dysphoria, every place becomes a danger zone. Entering school, you will see bullies and the stress gets to you. When you are going to a reunion with your family and you are forced to wear skirts that you don't like, the stress builds up on your muscles. When you report for work but your colleagues don't use the proper pronouns you want them to, you feel stress seeping out of your pores. Even when you are not in any imminent danger, the body still remembers the stress and this is felt as muscle tension.

Together with endurance of symptoms for 6 months and the impediment of these on function on important domains, we can diagnose anxiety as such. It can be tiring especially if you feel attacked all the time. People with gender dysphoria may feel that they need to explain many things about themselves to be accepted. And that can be worrying and anxious. If the mental condition persists, this can manifest somatically as cardiovascular diseases, palpitations, difficulty of breathing and a host of other medical conditions. All of these because you have worried unnecessarily.

Watch out for these danger signs. Depression and anxiety can attack many people but those with gender dysphoria are at a higher risk of contracting these illnesses. You have to recognize these symptoms and not dismiss them as normal. The more you misdiagnose or even not notice all of these abnormal behaviors, the longer it will take for any intervention and healing to take place.

Chapter 4: How to Overcome Depression and Anxiety

According to the Institute for Health Metrics Evaluation for 2017, mental disorders such as depression, is the third leading cause of disability. It will continue to grow in number through the next years. It is only now that governments are recognizing the importance of mental health on the overall health of individuals and of society in general. From early detection, we can mitigate the negative consequences of these disorders by initiating early interventions. Unlike medications, these interventions may take some time before the effect is seen. You may take Paracetamol for fever and you will feel that in a day, you are already afebrile. But when you consult for psychotherapy, you will only begin to see the effects on your mental health after a few sessions. Patience and a lot of dedication is needed if you truly want to be mentally healthy.

What we will outline here are just some of the ways you can address mental disorders stemming from gender dysphoria. Specifically, we will focus on addressing problems concerned with depression and anxiety. It is important for you to learn all of these steps because it may help you save a life of someone who might be undergoing an issue right now. You can also do these exercises on your own, even without a mental disorder. These exercises are meant to boost the overall mental health of all those who practice it. Don't just do these once or twice a week. Go through them every day of your life and you will feel healing becoming a habit and an antidote should you have any recurrences. The list is not exhaustive but contains an overview of the most current interventions of mental illness.

Recognize that you have a problem

This is the first step in any addiction program, the recognition of a problem. If you don't see that there is a problem, then no healing can take place. You have to realize that what you are experiencing is taking a toll on your social life, on your family, on your work, on your relationships with other people, on your physical and mental health. If you are too much into your thinking and stressing about which gender you should be, you cannot see anything else outside of that black hole. By observing your behavior and how it affects others, you will begin to be aware of your shortcomings. Recognize that you have a drinking problem because you don't want to think about the rejection of your loved ones on your preferred gender. Recognize that you have been cutting class or failing in school because you are bullied. Recognize that you have been slacking off at work and delivering shoddy work because you cannot concentrate. Recognize that the problem lies in you.

Denying won't get you anywhere. When you deny a problem, the more it will stink and degrade other aspects of your life. Denial is like putting rotten food in the fridge and not saying that it is there. You know that it will spoil the rest of the other food, but your pride is getting in your way. Also, stop blaming others. The natural tendency is really to put the blame on the other. Your boss is making your life hell. Your classmates are bullies. Your parents raised you in a gender you never wanted to be in. Maybe those are true. But you also had a part in making those conditions true. By your acceptance of the situation, you have let them get into you. The only change you can ever make is on yourself. You cannot change anymore how your mother dressed you in skirts when you wanted to wear pants. Stop blaming your teacher for giving you low marks in Math because you cannot concentrate in school. Stop whining altogether and accept responsibilities for your current situation. Only then can you start correcting your mistakes and living out the changes in yourself.

Meditate

Though this may be very simple, learning how to breathe can actually help you overcome anxiety and depression. It might be something we do on a daily basis, but there are actually ways on how to maximize breathing and use it to ease worrying and combat sadness. If you even try to be conscious of your breathing, you will realize how difficult it actually is to breathe. So perhaps it is better if I run you over one example of a breathing exercise for you to try out.

The prerequisite to this breathing exercise is to get a place and time where you can be quiet and free from all distractions. You can do it in the stillness of the early morning, in a break during the day or just before you go to sleep. Pick a place where you can be far away from your gadgets and phones, far from other people. This is your safe spot, a space where you can be free from all your stresses, free from the judgment of other people, free just to be yourself. If it helps you to concentrate, you can close your eyes.

And slowly, very, very slowly, breathe in. Let your breath come in for a full five seconds. Hold it for another five. Then breathe out very, very slowly for five seconds. Breathe in. Hold. Breathe out. Breathe in. Hold. Breathe out. Notice how the air is going through your nostrils, filling your nose and then exiting. Is it warm or cold? Are there smells you can notice? Dispel all thoughts from your head and just focus on the breath coming in and out of you. Notice every part of your body that is involved in breathing. Feel your chest rise and fall. Feel your nostrils opening and closing a bit. Feel how the air expands your chest and then relaxes it. Be conscious of everything that is involved in the act of breathing. And then, and only then, open your eyes. How do you feel? Are you more relaxed after this exercise? Do you feel energized after? Do this daily and you will really feel the benefits.

So what does breathing really do for you? There are several benefits that you can gain from being more conscious of how you breathe. First, breathing brings in quality air inside of you. When you breathe, you allow more oxygen to nourish your body especially your brain. When you feel anxious or depressed, there is less oxygen circulating in your body. The stress uses a lot of energy inside you and you feel weak and on edge because of this deprivation. Breathing will help bring oxygen to parts of your body that need it the most. This will help you think clearer and avoid impulsive behavior.

And second, you are able to redirect your attention from your stressors to a non-threatening stimulus such as breathing. Instead of worrying about an exam you have studied so much for, being more conscious about breathing relaxes your mind to optimize the learning. Instead of thinking how people may judge your decisions regarding your gender, breathing will calm you down. When you are anxious or depressed, you entertain a lot of negative thoughts about yourself, the world and the future. You are worried about things that are not yet happening. When you breathe, you forget all that. You are distracting your mind to focus on other things aside from those that stress you out. In this way, you avoid impulsive behavior. When you are stressed, you might feel a great pressure to react to situations which may not be good for you in the long run. A classmate bullies you for acting soft and feminine, so you punch him back. A workmate criticizes your hairstyle and refuses to call you proper pronouns so you pick a fight in the office. Not only would these resolve your issues, they would actually create more problems for you. When you focus on your breathing, you calm the body and prepare it to think about the best way you can deal with problems. When you feel relaxed, you will be able to think better about alternatives and best options in resolving issues. So be generous about breathing and be conscious of this life-saving act. The better breather you are, the better thinker and the more positive disposition you will adopt.

Daily routine

When you hit a difficult part in your life, it is very hard to bounce back. Especially for gender dysphoric people, they will encounter a lot of challenges from their own selves, from their family, workmates and society in general. Not many people will be able to understand what they are going through and dismiss their thoughts and behavior as queer and deviant. There is a big tendency to withdraw altogether from socializing and from work as you try to preserve yourself. You may be in so much pain that you just want to rest and be alone. This is understandable given the circumstances. But by withdrawing from important domains of your life, you risk developing depression.

How do you bounce from depression? It is good to keep to a schedule, a daily routine. In your better days, you should already establish a certain pattern of activities throughout the day. You have to wake up at around the same time. Plan what course of actions come first. Do you take a bath first, eat breakfast next, and then relieve your toilet urges? In the morning, establish the routine for going to work, timing in and proceeding to the orders for the day. Eat meals on time, never skipping because you don't feel like it. The evenings can be more spontaneous because there might be a lot of events you really can't prepare for. But allot some time for evening events and then make your evening rest regular. Sleep also on time so your body will be able to wake up and start the cycle anew. Keep this routine every day with much religiosity.

How does routine actually combat anxiety and depression? When you do a routine, you are able to anticipate a sequence of events that will actually happen. This helps you get a grasp over the unpredictability of a day. You will feel more anxious if you don't know what will happen tomorrow or the next day. When you do a routine, there is a semblance of order that you can look forward to and lessen your anxiety. You may not be able to prepare for everything and predict what will happen 100% accurately. But when you do a routine, you have some inkling as to what things may occur in the future time. It will help you calm down knowing that you will eat lunch at this hour. It will ease your mind if you know that you will go home at this particular time. You will feel better having a fixed amount of sleep. Just don't overdo it in the sense that you panic when a certain order is not met. Anxiety will increase if you follow a routine that will not allow for variations and adjustments. You don't really know what may occur during the day, whether you will have many clients and appointments throughout the afternoon and you can rest awhile. Make a routine that will make allowances for other activities.

In terms of depression, routine will give you something to look forward to. Instead of sleeping longer hours and wallowing in self-pity, the routine will force you to brush your teeth, eat your breakfast and go to your work. There is a counterforce that drives you away from your negative tendencies to something that is productive. When you have made the routine a habit, you will actually not think about the process consciously and just let your body go through the motions. When you keep on moving in a routine, you will find it easier to focus less on your stressors and more on the actual things you are doing. Instead of isolating yourself in your room, the routine gets you out of bed to continue your daily living. You will really feel how routines can be lifesaving especially if you are undergoing a painful transition.

Keep in touch with friends and family

They may have hurt you as you try to make them understand your identity. They may have judged you and be sources of discrimination for you. But they are your friends and family. At the end of the day, they love you, more than their shortcomings. When you feel depressed, you just want to cut yourself from all your social contacts. By isolating yourself, you increase your depression because you feel more alone with your problems. It is difficult to let them understand, but the solution is never to cut people off and ostracize yourself from the public sphere.

You may not need a lot of friends, but you can pick friends you trust and value. These people will love you through your painful moments, be there when you need help and give the strength to go through the day. When you have much incongruence with who you really are, emotional support from family and friends is critical. You need to understand that your problems are never yours alone, both in the experiencing and in the resolving. If you think that you are hurt by negative comments, people who care for you are also hurt in your pain. If you think that you are alone when you feel misjudged by people, people who love you are also hurt for you. What you feel is never only personal. It will also hurt other people when you withdraw from them. So share your pain. Share the burden you feel because you don't need to carry it alone. Many people are afraid of unloading to others about their pain because they feel they will not be understood. Try them. They may not understand 100% now, but eventually, they will. What is good is that they tried to reach out to you and make you feel that you are not alone.

A good friend is also important in giving you quality feedback. They can mirror to you if your opinions about the world and yourself are actually true. They can reflect back to you the behaviors they observe which you keep on doing but are actually paining you. We all have our blind spots, areas in our lives where we cannot see clearly or at all. We need somebody else to mirror our behavior to ourselves. Our friends are the best people for that. They will be able to tell you the tough truth you need to hear because they care for you. Left to ourselves, we may be self-preserving and defensive, always thinking that we are right the whole time. A person we trust will give us another perspective that is different and also true about the reality we see. You may be so consumed with your gender identity that you close yourself to the opinions of others. A friend may help you remedy that blind spot and allow you to have a broader perspective on things.

Find a hobby

Find something outside of work or school or your main activities that will give you pleasure. This may be an old habit you have not done for a long time. You have been holed up in your room or in the office, sulking for yourself. Try revisiting an old past time. This may be an old passion like photography that you have not tried out for a long time. You may have enjoyed cooking before but have not found the time; just take up the pan and cook again. You may have enjoyed painting; get your brush again and start on a new canvass. Or it could be a new passion altogether. If you have not tried wall-climbing, why not start now? If you have only dreamt about motor cross racing, then try doing it today. If you have always been curious about diving, take those gears out now and start exploring the sea. Finding a hobby is one of the best remedies for anxiety and depression.

How do hobbies help you exactly? One, as with breathing, hobbies interrupt the negative spiraling process of your depression and anxiety. If you have been too involved in your quest for identity and recognition and you only get rejection left and right, why not give it a rest and try something different? The more you push an agenda, the more elusive it will be because you may not be thinking correctly at this point. So you have to get out of your box, away from your usual comfort zone and try engaging in a totally new experience. When you are doing something that gives you pleasure, you are stimulating endorphins to be released into your system, driving away the depressive mood. You are also stimulating other parts of the brain that will help you either deflect from your current preoccupation or broaden your perspective. In pursuing hobbies, you might even find some resolution in the incongruence you are feeling.

Instead of focusing on the gender issue as your central problem, you may begin to be consumed with a different passion altogether.

We also want to watch out for substance abuse which gender dysphoric patients have an increased propensity to engage in. These are bad habits you should not try at all if you are depressive or anxious. You may become dependent on these substances, goading you to increase dosages to get your high and eventually overwhelm your system and kill you. You need to find more wholesome and productive avenues to gain the pleasure you need to cope with your stressors. By engaging in hobbies, you will still get your high but in a more organic, sustainable and life-giving way.

Exercise

You may be surprised but exercising actually helps you fight off depression and anxiety. It will directly benefit you because the more you move your body, the healthier hormones will be released. When you are stressed from facing your internal struggles, you can get stuck with an overdose of norepinephrine and adrenaline, the 'fight or flight' hormones. They are in charge of priming your body to meet with any attack. The longer they stay in your body that is not necessarily used, the more damage they can deal especially in your cardiovascular and muscular system. When you exercise, you allow hormones to circulate in your system. Oxygen is carried to all the tissues of your body, giving them the necessary replenishment they need. Blood flow will also take out the toxins in your body which are harmful when they pool up. Exercise will also facilitate the release of endorphins or your happy hormones which will combat depression.

The exercise need not be something as intense as a marathon. That could count if you are really into that sport. But any simple activity that will allow you to sweat is a great health boost. Running or brisk walking, walking with a friend is better, will suffice to improve blood flow. There are activities which have a protective factor to your joints such as swimming or yoga. Zumba or aerobics combines the stimulation of movement and music which improves your body's condition doubly. You may engage in these exercises for 30 minutes three times a week and that would be enough to achieve a good flow in your body and strength for your muscles.

Exercise will also benefit you from the harmful effects of depression and anxiety. One of the factors that are included in the diagnosis of these is too much or too little eating. When you exercise, you also consume the energy that you have eaten, so you limit the fats you accumulate. The act of moving will also stimulate leptin, a biochemical, that will make you feel satiated so you don't eat as much. In exercise, you can lessen the risk of obesity and the cardiovascular disorder that go with a sedentary lifestyle. Having gender dysphoria must not limit you in exploring other parts of your body and personality that are also important. Your physical health will nurture your mental health. Even if you have an issue with gender, a good body can be a good environment for more level thinking.

Seek help

The biggest enemy of all mental disorders is the ego. It is that part of us which thinks of ourselves as superior and faultless. When we have a strong ego, we cannot accept our weakness and our need for another person to help us. When you start recognizing that you have a problem, this should segue way into a realization that you cannot help yourself alone. When you have a mental illness, it is not a matter of willing to change. In reality, these schemes never work because a sick person cannot really help themselves.

Seek the help that you need. This is a humbling recognition that you are not perfect and that at this point in your life, you need someone to direct you in the right path. Help may be in the form of a psychologist or a psychiatrist who can assess your problem objectively and form intervention programs fitted for your condition. What is good with psychiatry is that it recognizes that mental health is not a cognitive or abstract activity. Much of the mental illnesses we encounter are actually biochemical imbalances triggered by life events. As such, you may not actually have control over your body. When stressed, the body will release stress hormones all over and this will affect your entire person, from the physical aspect, to the mood, the personality, the thought and actions you will make. But there are some people whose biochemical imbalances cannot be corrected naturally. When you have depressed or anxious states for a prolonged period of time, the body is exposed extensively to hormones that can already affect semi-permanently your physiology. Hence, psychiatrist will use medications, fighting biochemical hormones with biochemical interventions. If you need to sleep, there are drugs that will help you sleep. If you feel panicky, there are medications that will make you feel calm. If you feel down, there are medications that will lift your spirit momentarily. You cannot access these medications unless you consult your doctor. In my opinion, overcoming these issues naturally by doing the exercises I mentioned previously is better than medication. However, medication for other issues related to the body as a result of being depressed for a long time is recommended. For example, you may have been engaged in overconsumption of alcohol and you acquired a liver disease, or you may have been smoking and you now experience trouble with breathing.

Professionals would also be the best people to consult regarding your condition. They have studied a long time just to understand these mental illnesses and how to treat them. Aside from medications, there are also a host of other therapies that are available depending on the openness of a person. Cognitive behavioral therapy would involve a more self-reflective approach, where the therapist would draw out insights from a client on their thoughts and behaviors, mirroring how these interact and helping the person change both. Art therapy would use drawings and craft materials to both elicit subliminal repressed feelings and also heal the person through the process. Psychotherapy would draw out from the unconscious elements from the past or the present which may affect to subconscious processes of a person that they would need to confront. These therapies will only be effective if handled properly and given to the right people. There is help to those who will seek it.

Chapter 5: Prevention and Treatment of Gender Dysphoria

Having discussed the co-morbid mental illnesses associated with gender dysphoria, we also have to tackle the all-important issue itself. We have to take note that these mental illnesses may co-exist and may feed off each other. Anxiety, depression and gender dysphoria may be the cause and the effect and the sustaining factor of each other. Hence, treatment in one aspect will also affect the other mental illness. If you are exercising to ward off depression, that will also benefit your anxiety and your gender dysphoria.

The effect may not be direct, but it will contribute to the general well-being of a person.

The primary intervention for gender dysphoria is of course prevention. But this is a controversial topic because we don't really know how we can totally prevent gender dysphoria from happening. Instead, you have to recognize the causes of gender dysphoria. We have enumerated several factors such as genetics, environment and culture. There are not a lot of studies about genetics so that is an area we can least focus on. And because it is genetics, there is not much we can do in the passing of genes when we try to control for certain traits like gender dysphoria. The factors then that we can focus on really are the environment and the culture or society. We can actively change these domains so that people will experience less of gender dysphoria.

First, the environment in the family sets the tone on how mental illnesses from personal issues are going to develop. If you have an atmosphere in the house that is very hostile, that is very totalitarian, children will not feel safe to explore themselves or voice out their opinions. Yes, there is a concern for forming children according to the norms of society. As parents, we have a duty to raise our kids in the best way possible. But the home environment should also be nurturing in terms of questions about sexuality and identity. There is less stigma for gender dysphoric individuals when they are raised in families who are open to discussion and have created spaces for communication. As parents, you may not agree with the choices and preferences of your children. But that should not stop you from communicating with them, from hearing their opinion and giving your own advice. Children are still at a malleable age where they can be formed, so parents have the supreme duty in instilling a sense of openness and safety regarding gender issues.

Culture is more difficult to change because it is resistant but not invulnerable to change. We have seen historically how perspectives change, how norms on what it means to be male and female have developed. You have to realize that these changes happen across time. Women were only able to vote after a half century of male dominance and neglect for the rights of women. If you want to be an advocate of gender openness, it will not happen overnight or even in our lifetime. You only open yourself to a lot of rejection and hopelessness when you set too high expectations on the changes you want to enact in society. But, we have to emphasize that changes happen across minute acts of indignation. To be accepted for the gender you prefer may not occur overnight, but little acts will go a long way. You can start by engaging people in conversation about gender identity. You need not be defensive or preachy the whole time because it will really turn off a lot of people who do not want change. Instead, go and make friends you can share your opinions to. When they see your cause and how passionate you are in asserting your true identity, they will pass it off to others, setting a ripple of changes. If you want to correct people around you regarding the use of appropriate pronouns, check first if they are open to that. You cannot force yourself and your truth to everybody. You have to respect that they have their own opinions too and may not be ready for the kind of truth you want to tell them. Be gentle as you advocate for gender identity.

Prevention can go a long way in controlling the prevalence of gender dysphoria. But we still don't have sufficient and exhaustive evidences on the causes of gender dysphoria that is why we also include treatment interventions for those who have gender dysphoria. Again, it may be tiring to repeat that we are not curing being gay or being lesbian or having a transgender identity. These are not mental illness to begin with. Instead, we want to control the negative effects of dysphoria in persons struggling with their gender identity.

Like depression and anxiety, the first step is the recognition of the problem. You have to accept that you are undergoing increase and debilitating stress because of your gender issue. The more you deny that thinking about your gender has a crippling effect on your work and performance, the longer it takes to give you the intervention you need. Recognize that what you are feeling and thinking and behaving has an impact on different aspects of your life and that you need help. Not everyone who has a gender issue has gender dysphoria. For some, it concerns them, but they are able to function well at social events and at work. But for those who have been diagnosed with the disorder, the gender issue has severely affected them for a long time that they cannot help themselves.

And again, the next step is to seek professional help. There are psychiatrists who have been trained to handle patients with gender dysphoria. If you think that you are the only one who is confused with identity or who feels don't identify with one's anatomy, think again. These experts have come across a lot of individuals, have performed and read a lot of researches, and have managed a lot of gender dysphoric patients. They may be able to prescribe you medications when you feel anxious about a certain event. They can give you medications to help you sleep so that you feel rested when you are stressed. They might control symptoms of schizophrenia by giving you drugs to ward off these hallucinations. Psychiatrists may be the best help you can get in order to manage your own dysphoria.

There are also a lot of support groups for gender dysphoria. Groups like ParentsofROGDkids (Rapid Onset Gender Dysphoria), The Trevor Project, LGBTQ+ Youth, etc. were developed to bring together individuals with the disorder. By sharing with others your own stories and struggles, there is already healing happening. When you realize that you are not alone in your struggles, then the incongruence becomes bearable. Social support from people who understand you and will not judge you is essential to people struggling with gender dysphoria. The safety net provided by a support group will help ward off suicidal ideation and attempts and even just bouts of depression. These groups may even be sources of advocacy. Because you all believe in the same advocacy, you can let others know about your gender identity and the struggle to live out your preferred gender. As a group, you can launch campaigns for other people to also understand your issue. In this way, you are creating small pockets of change that may eventually affect the gender restrictive culture we are living in.

There are also more medical and surgical measures to address the dysphoria. The core issue of a gender dysphoric person is the desire to be rid of one's anatomical parts and the desire for obtaining the other gender's primary and sexual characteristics. Body modifications may help, but not totally alleviate gender dysphoria. We have to remember that the struggle is actually just in the mind. The intervention then should target the mind and how we think about the situation. This is where therapy and psychiatry come in. But the mind may also be aided by physical or corporal cues. By changing the body, we help the mind resolve the incongruence it experiences.

The more conservative approach is of course the medical modification. This involves the intake of hormones that will enhance the secondary characteristics of your preferred gender. We have to reiterate that because this is a medical modification, only a licensed doctor can give you the prescription. If you only self-medicate and Google your way to the pharmacy, you may be opening yourself to unwanted side effects. So, if you are determined to undergo hormone therapy, you have to be supervised by a licensed doctor.

Hair, breast, voice changes, and body physique are all controlled by hormones in our body. These are sex specific. Males will have a lot of androgen from the production of testosterone from their scrotum. Females will have a majority of estrogen produced from their ovaries. But both men and women have these hormones. The main difference is really the amount of hormones predominant in an individual. The effect of testosterone is masculinizing. If you have a lot of testosterone, you develop facial, axillary, pubic and body hair. Women too have hair because of testosterone, but not as much as males. Testosterone also induces the lowering of voices and the aggression in males. Estrogen on the other hand induces the development of breasts and the pitch of females. Males will also produce some estrogen though to a lesser degree.

Hormone therapy then involves the induction of hormones on an individual. For those wishing to be more female, estrogen is either induced or given. For those wishing to be males, testosterone is induced or given. The primary target of hormone therapy then is the development of the secondary characteristics. There is a feminizing or masculinizing effect seen in patients when levels increase beyond the normal. Males wishing to be females may see breast buds and a thinning of the voice. Females who wish to be males will have hair outgrowth like beards and sideburns. Hormone therapy may be lifelong if you want to retain the sexual characteristics of the opposite gender. It may be pricey and also prolonged. But a caveat is warranted. You cannot simply take these medications without consulting a doctor. There are serious side effects to taking these hormones. Estrogen for example can also cause obesity, blood clots that can lead to stroke, and even breast cancer.

The more radical approach is, of course, the surgical. This is reserved for those who have a very intense desire to obtain the primary and secondary sexual characteristics of the opposite gender and have the means to go about it. Surgical procedures may range from plastic reconstruction of breasts to the cutting out of the primary sex organs to the creation of new sexual organs. Modifications may be simple cosmetic procedures especially for those who may want to appear more feminine or masculine. Or they could be as radical as sexual reassignment surgeries. Surgical procedures are often very definite. Patients have to undergo intense psychological screening before they can be admitted for these procedures. Physicians would want to be very sure that these are the procedures you really desire because it will be difficult to undo the surgery. There is also intense psychological therapy after the procedure. Patients have to be counseled and processed with the physical changes that have happened to them. Some may be very satisfied with the results. A small majority feel some sense of regret at their decision. Hence, people with gender dysphoria should really consider if surgery will really reduce their distress. A lot of preparation and reflection must accompany individuals who wish to have surgical reassignment.

Conclusion

Gender dysphoria continues to affect a lot of people who may not be satisfied with their given gender. They will always be longing for the other gender, to be treated as the other, to have the sexual organs and characteristics of the other, to be the other gender. What you are experiencing is a real concern and should be addressed. Be informed of what gender dysphoria is and how it develops as you grow old. Take care of your mental health because people with gender dysphoria are very prone to a lot of co-morbid illnesses like depression and anxiety. Explore a range of treatments that may help alleviate your distress. You are very special and know that no matter what gender you choose, you are beautiful inside and out. Hopefully, this book has helped you through the confusing, depressing, lonely road of gender dysphoria. Though you can never really eradicate it, this book is a testament that you are not alone in your journey. There are a lot of people experiencing what you are going through and we all need to look out for each other. The world may be very judging and discriminating. But instead of clamming up and retreating, you should do little acts of indignation in order to change the society we live in to one that is more gender-sensitive and open. May this book be your guide in the exciting journey towards your true self.

Leave a Review

As an independent author with a small marketing budget, reviews are my livelihood on this platform. If you enjoyed this book, I'd really appreciate your honest feedback. You can do so by leaving a review on this book's page on Amazon. I love hearing from my readers and I personally read every single review.

www.ingramcontent.com/pod-product-compliance
Lightning Source LLC
Chambersburg PA
CBHW051213250726
48655CB00006B/2388